T. Harri Jones
1921-1965

Editor: Pat Power
Co-editors: P. Bernard Jones, Liz Felgate

*Bernard
Jones Best
Wishes*

X y y

Welsh Arts Council 1987

Foreword

T. Harri Jones' comparatively short life took him from his childhood in mid-Wales to England, Scotland, the Mediterranean, Africa, and finally into a sometimes bitter exile in Australia. In his poetry Harri drew extensively on his memories of the first eighteen years of his life in remote Breconshire. As a young adult he romantically fictionalised himself as a 'poor boy from the hills' who escaped from claustrophobia and poverty to eventual success as a famous poet. The fiction almost became reality.

Harri is important in twentieth-century Anglo-Welsh literature because it was as a rural poet that he worked out his ambivalent relationship with Wales: a Wales that educated him out of his class into what eventually became, for Harri, the sterility of a career as an exiled academic. Distanced from the source of his poetry, he envisaged a return to Wales as his salvation.

Together with R.S. Thomas, Harri was the major Anglo-Welsh poet of the interregnum that occured between the death of Dylan Thomas and the 'second flowering' of Anglo-Welsh literature in the mid-1960s. His death in Australia in 1965 cut short his key contribution to this emerging movement.

To mark the twentieth anniversary of Harri's death in 1985, Ben Jones was commissioned by the Welsh Sculpture Trust to provide a sculpture in Builth Wells for the Powys Sculpture Trail. To coincide with this event, we produced an exhibition on 'The Life and Times of T. Harri Jones': this book has been developed from the exhibition originally shown at Wyeside Arts Centre.

In attempting to explain Harri and his world this book emphasises the rich variety of his family background, with many personal photographs from Pat Power's collection, identifying the gallery of real people and places that figure in Harri's poetry.

Harri, with his well-developed sense of fun, would have found the whole exercise rather amusing.

Pat Power   P. Bernard Jones   Liz Felgate

Pat Power, P. Bernard Jones, Liz Felgate

1. T. Harri Jones' family tree.

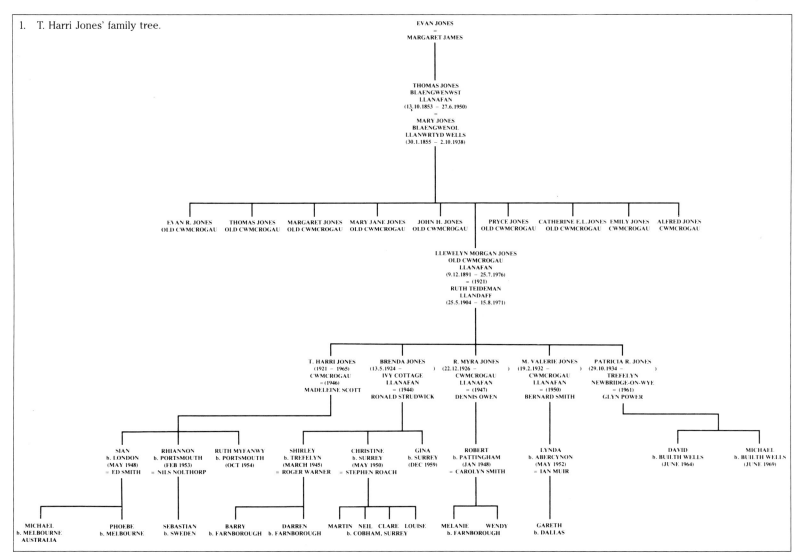

EVAN JONES
=
MARGARET JAMES

THOMAS JONES
BLAENGWENWST
LLANAFAN
(13.10.1853 – 27.6.1950)
=
MARY JONES
BLAENGWENOL
LLANWRTYD WELLS
(30.1.1855 – 2.10.1938)

EVAN R. JONES OLD CWMCROGAU
THOMAS JONES OLD CWMCROGAU
MARGARET JONES OLD CWMCROGAU
MARY JANE JONES OLD CWMCROGAU
JOHN H. JONES OLD CWMCROGAU
PRYCE JONES OLD CWMCROGAU
CATHERINE E.L. JONES OLD CWMCROGAU
EMILY JONES CWMCROGAU
ALFRED JONES CWMCROGAU

LLEWELYN MORGAN JONES
OLD CWMCROGAU
LLANAFAN
(9.12.1891 – 25.7.1976)
= (1921)
RUTH TEIDEMAN
LLANDAFF
(25.5.1904 – 15.8.1971)

T. HARRI JONES
(1921 – 1965)
CWMCROGAU
= (1946)
MADELEINE SCOTT

BRENDA JONES
(13.5.1924 –)
IVY COTTAGE
LLANAFAN
= (1944)
RONALD STRUDWICK

R. MYRA JONES
(22.12.1926 –)
CWMCROGAU
LLANAFAN
= (1947)
DENNIS OWEN

M. VALERIE JONES
(19.2.1932 –)
CWMCROGAU
LLANAFAN
= (1950)
BERNARD SMITH

PATRICIA R. JONES
(29.10.1934 –)
TREFELYN
NEWBRIDGE-ON-WYE
= (1961)
GLYN POWER

SIAN
b. LONDON
(MAY 1948)
= ED SMITH

RHIANNON
b. PORTSMOUTH
(FEB 1953)
= NILS NOLTHORP

RUTH MYFANWY
b. PORTSMOUTH
(OCT 1954)

SHIRLEY
b. TREFELYN
(MARCH 1945)
= ROGER WARNER

CHRISTINE
b. SURREY
(MAY 1950)
= STEPHEN ROACH

GINA
b. SURREY
(DEC 1959)

ROBERT
b. PATTINGHAM
(JAN 1948)
= CAROLYN SMITH

LYNDA
b. ABERCYNON
(MAY 1952)
= IAN MUIR

DAVID
b. BUILTH WELLS
(JUNE 1964)

MICHAEL
b. BUILTH WELLS
(JUNE 1969)

MICHAEL
b. MELBOURNE
AUSTRALIA

PHOEBE
b. MELBOURNE

SEBASTIAN
b. SWEDEN

BARRY
b. FARNBOROUGH

DARREN
b. FARNBOROUGH

MARTIN NEIL CLARE LOUISE
b. COBHAM, SURREY

MELANIE WENDY
b. FARNBOROUGH

GARETH
b. DALLAS

Where we were born, a windy place,
A broken landscape of regrets,
High curlews calling, the careful men
Nursed their rocky memories in silence,
Avoiding the fat plains and their brute inhabitants.

'Ancestral'

3. Harri's country.

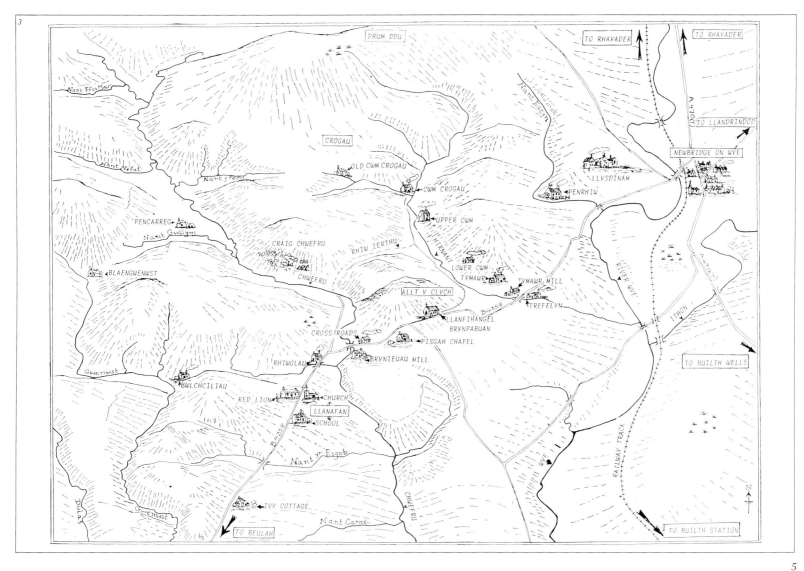

4.   Henry Teideman, Harri's maternal grandfather, was born in 1864, the Cockney son of a whaler. He ran away from home and became a lion-tamer and bare-fist fighter with Lord John Sanger's Circus — he achieved fame by fighting kangaroos. He moved to Porth in South Wales where, according to family tradition, his pugilistic skills were put to good use as a bodyguard to Arthur Cook, the miners' leader. In Porth he met and married Rhoda Jones, a Welsh-speaking girl from the Rhondda, who introduced him to the Salvation Army. Henry was a coal merchant in Barry until his business collapsed in the Depression owing to his generosity.

4b

4a

5a

5. Ruth Teideman, Harri's mother, standing on a wall behind her uncle, was born in 1904. She left school at thirteen, and went into service in a boys' school in Halifax. Ruth and Lily had fourteen brothers and sisters, none of whom spoke Welsh.

5b

6

6. Thomas and Mary Jones, Harri's paternal grandparents, were born and brought up in North Breconshire. The area was one of farms and small-holdings scattered over the foothills and valleys that ran into a huge expanse of empty, open country. Thomas was born at Blaengwenwst farm, Llanafan Fawr, and in the 1871 census, when he was twelve years of age, he was entered as a 'scholar'. Mary was born at Blaengwenol, Llanwrtyd Wells. Both Thomas and Mary were Welsh-speakers.

7. When Thomas and Mary married they moved to Cwm Crogau, a thirty-four-acre smallholding on the Llysdinam estate owned by the Venables-Llewellyn family. Thomas became known as 'Crogau'. The small holding, 1,000 feet above sea-level, was one of the many moorland-edge farms in the area bordering the thousands of acres of common land stretching beyond Abergwesyn to the west, and over to the Elan Valley to the north. Thomas was a shepherd on the estate, and a rate collector for the Council. The annual rent for Cwm Crogau was £12 and Thomas earned £36.16s as a shepherd. He was a keen Congregationalist and taught the Welsh-speakers of Llanafan English for a penny a night in the loft above the stable of Pisgah Chapel.

Under God's violent unsleeping eye
My fathers laboured for three hundred years
On the same farm, in the expected legend.

'Difference'

8. Llysdinam Hall

8

9

9. Thomas and Mary had ten surviving children. Their sixth child, Llewelyn Morgan Jones (back row, second from the left), was Harri's father. He was born at Cwm Crogau in 1891.

10

10. Shortly after Llew's birth a new home (also named Cwm Crogau) was built near the track running the length of the Hirnant valley.

11. Llew was a dapper young man.
His ambition was to become a
chauffeur and whilst learning to drive
in 1912, he posed in the car of a
passing encyclopaedia salesman on
'The Groe' — Builth Wells' municipal
park. In November 1914 he enlisted
with the Glamorgan Yeomanry and
served in Egypt, Palestine and France.

11b

11a

12

12.   Conscious that he would photograph better without his hat, Llew gathered with other survivors of the Great War from the Newbridge-on-Wye area.

All honour to Cwm Crogau's son,
  The shepherd from the hill,
Who readily answered England's call
  With a determined will.
Like him, the boys of Afan's hill
  Will join the fighting line,
To do their share for hearth and home,
  Where England's banners shine.

From Cribyn's top to Capel Rhos
  We whisper (not in fun),
We'll save old England from a fall
  And crush the cruel Hun.
Let's leave our flocks upon the hills
  To graze and prance at ease,
In place of crook we'll take the sword
  For freedom and for peace.

Brecon County Times (1914)
Doggerel by a 'Llanafan Lad'.

13. On his return from the war, Llew sought work in South Wales, where he met his future wife, Ruth Teideman, in Porth in 1920.

'Hannah was seventeen: short, fair, not quite plump, very ready to be amused, very ready to be warm and loving to everybody...

Hannah met Iago on the street and loved him from the moment she saw him. He was very dark and quiet, a man from the mountains, not at ease in the brightness and cheer of the towns. He had been a boy just starting to plough four years ago when some obscure impulse had made him volunteer; now he was a man older than he should have been. He talked very little, and hardly at all about his war experiences. This gave him an air of reserve and mystery. Hannah, like all her family and practically everybody she knew, talked all the time, with a bright, not very intelligent, babbling cheerfulness. Iago's moody silence, the brusque intermittence of his conversation, fascinated her almost as much as his alien physical quality held her blood in unquestioning desire.'

'Home'

14

14. Following their marriage, Llew took Ruth back to Llanafan Fawr to live at Cwm Crogau with his parents. To Ruth, Cwm Crogau seemed very remote, in stark contrast to the industrial community of the Rhondda. Allt-y-clych, the distinctive hill at the entrance of the Hirnant valley, dominated the landscape from Cwm Crogau.

'Iago's home was only forty miles away; but she knew little about that country or about his family. The loneliness and the bareness and the silence had terrified her from the beginning, and the Welsh-speaking hill people, withdrawn, clannish, sly, were like foreigners. From the first moment she was an exile, an outsider, not welcomed or wanted. Iago remained mysterious, remote: his reserved silence became sullenness, and the brutality with which he had first taken her became the norm of his behaviour.'

'Home'

15. Llew became a roadman with Breconshire County Council.

16a

16. Thomas Henry Jones (Harri) was Llew and Ruth's first child. He was delivered by a midwife who smoked a clay pipe, at Cwm Crogau on 21st December, 1921. Shortly after Harri was born, Llew's elder brother Jack married and Llew and Ruth had to move to Ivy Cottage in Llanafan. Brenda, seen here with Harri (16a), was born in this house, which is now a ruin (16b). When Jack went to live in Hirwaun in 1924, they returned home to Cwm Crogau. Llew never taught his children to speak Welsh.

16b

17a   Pencarreg

17b   Penrhiw

But to us who were born above Pencarreg
Head in the clouds is true, is simply true.
Nor all the brazen comfort of the sun
Can dissipate the clouds upon Penrhiw.

'Head in the Clouds'

18.   Dan and Flora Jones. Dan was Harri's great uncle and lived at Bwlchciliau, another Llanafan farm. Dan was a Welsh-speaker and local bard: his *englynion* were famous in the district. On seeing his great nephew for the first time, Dan predicted Harri would be a poet.

. . . See Daniel wear the sky
Like a sodden overcoat, the earth weighing down
His feet, as he wrestles again with an old text
And wonders why his sheep are so obstinate about dying.
Sometimes, picking stones off an old, thin field,
Or riding, wet to the waist, through the bracken
In search of old, thin sheep scarce worth the saving,
His mind would be lifted from perverse sons and daughters,
His head kestrelled in space towards Allt-y-clych,
And he felt he could prophesy like Isaiah.

'In Memoriam'

19a

19a   Brenda and Harri

The wideawake sky went on for ever and ever
Over my boyhood, the eternal trees
Denied the fear of death, the flowers in their seasons
Were all immortal, and the birds sang
As everlastingly as the grass enchanted.

Tall men, tall women, went walking like trees
On my blue horizons, and catkin children
Swung in adventurous breezes to the tunes
Behind the chapels and cowsheds, the tunes
Of ferns and grasses, of druidic trees.

'The Ballad of Me'

19b

20. The Cwm Crogau small-holding, with its sheep, cows, a pig, chickens and a vegetable garden, involved all the Jones family. Old Mrs Jones' sight was failing by the time Harri was born, but she remained the matriarch.

. . . See Mary Jane, tiny
And eighty, who's had ten children, and milked
The cows immediately before and after
Each birth.

'Portrait Gallery'

21. Auntie Lily, from Porth, visited her sister at Cwm Crogau.

22. Llew and friends.

23. Llew, Ruth, Brenda and Harri at Cwm Crogau.

24a

24.   Life was difficult for Ruth: she had to cope with Llew's moods, his fondness for a pint and living with her in-laws. She was well liked by her neighbours, but at one time life at Cwm Crogau became too much to bear and she travelled back to Porth with the children. However, Brenda missed her father and after a week they returned. In 1926, Ruth's second daughter, Myra, was born (24a). At this time, domestic life in the Llanafan area was hard. Every Tuesday, Ruth struggled up the valley on foot from Llanfihangel Brynpabuan with the groceries, whilst on Fridays she rode the eight miles to Llandrindod Wells to sell her butter and eggs. At Cwm Crogau water was brought in from the well each night; the house was lit by candle and oil lamp; there was no wireless, and the *tŷ bach* straddled the small stream that ran down the Crogau valley.

24b

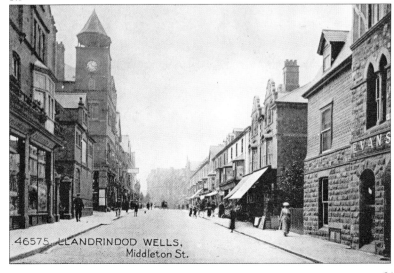

46575. LLANDRINDOD WELLS,
Middleton St.

25.   Harri, Brenda and Myra were fortunate in receiving toys from their grandparents in South Wales. The two eldest children played with their neighbours' children at Upper Cwm — a quarter of a mile down the valley. The boys at Upper Cwm called Brenda 'Blackbird': she was their favourite because they had no sister of their own.

'. . . they would say when neighbours or relatives commented on the pony shyness of my manners or the wildness of my eyes, Oh, he's the old man's boy. We can't do much with him.'

'My Grandfather would have me be a Poet.'

25b

25a

26

26.   Despite its remote location, Cwm Crogau never lacked visitors.

27

27.   Auntie Maggie, Llew's spinster sister who lived with the three children at Cwm Crogau, was the owner of a box camera, and she took many of these early photographs.

'. . . Auntie, the virgin old before her time, scraggy as an old wether, the daughter sacrificed to the parents as the parents had themselves been sacrificed to their children.'

'Home'

28a

28. Thomas (fifth from the left) was one of the founder members of the Llanafan Sheep Dog Trials held in the fields around the Red Lion Inn. Harri was known as 'Crogau's grandson' rather than Llew's son. Each Monday Harri caught the pony, Bess, for Thomas who rode to Newbridge-on-Wye to catch the train to Builth Wells where he spent market day drinking in the Swan public house and collecting the rates for the Council.

28b

> *. . . The old names still resound*
> *For me of farms, men, ponies, dogs,*
> *The old names that are all that I possess*
> *Of my own language, proud then*
> *And prouder now to call myself only*
> *Young Crogau, old Crogau's grandson.*

'My Grandfather Going Blind'

29. At this time, the labour-intensive nature of farming drew the community together. Everyone ploughed with horses. Although the Cwm Crogau fields were never ploughed, Llew worked with horses in the neighbourhood.

29a

29b

—You have to plough the furrows I have ploughed,
Or pick the stones off the bitter fields
Before they're fit for ploughing, all day, all day,
Or lift potatoes until your back is breaking,
And then go home to the grudged candlelight
And the green bacon—you want your childhood
Spent like that—and that with the compensations:
An old man's voice like something out of Daniel
Making the Belshazzars of the tractors tremble,
Hills, like Mam's breasts, homely and tremendous,
Schooled wildness of sheepdogs, ponnies stubborn
As myself, and each winter's killing snow.

'The Welshman in Exile Speaks'

30. Oats were cut by scythe and stooked by hand on the slopes of Allt-y-clych.

31. Brenda (far right) often helped her neighbours, the Davies family, at Lower Cwm.

32. At Cwm Crogau, haymaking involved all the family.

'. . . *You must believe*
In some impossibly glorious promise
To mow meadows and milk cows in such
Unlikely places.'

'Cwmchwefri'

33a

33b

33. Young people from Pisgah Chapel were baptised in the Chwefru beside Brynieuau Mill.

Suppose—this is the moment when your scream
Awakes you to your own sweat and dirt—suppose
You had let yourself be dipped in the Chwefru
(Below where the trout were, and where they washed the sheep) . . . .

'Spoiled Preacher'

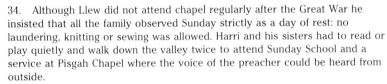

34. Although Llew did not attend chapel regularly after the Great War he insisted that all the family observed Sunday strictly as a day of rest: no laundering, knitting or sewing was allowed. Harri and his sisters had to read or play quietly and walk down the valley twice to attend Sunday School and a service at Pisgah Chapel where the voice of the preacher could be heard from outside.

And the capel, God in a little bwthin
Once whitewashed—but God in the voices
Of the mean, the crippled, the green bacon eaters,
The lead me beside still waters buggers, the wild boys,
The sin-eaters, and the godly daughters,
All of them suddenly in unison
In the ugliest building I have ever seen
—Pisgah I shall never see again—

'The Welshman in Exile Speaks'

35. The Reverend Davies (seen here with relations and friends of Harri's grandparents) was known as 'Jelly Belly' because he always chose to visit his parishoners at meal times.

36a

36. In 1926 Harri became a pupil at Llanafan Church School: he walked the three miles with the boys from Upper Cwm, often day-dreaming and bird-nesting. The route took them over the 'short cut' of Rhiw Ierthi, the wild path that climbs to 1,100 feet, dropping down into the Chwefru Valley, past the old oak to the footbridge and then on to school.

Back to the loved sky and the humped hills,
The night-infested woods, the fish-cold brooks,
Pride of the fox and buzzard, all lonely terror
Of empty winds over Wales.
My fronded boyhood breaking like a tide
Flung up all contraries, the five gay kingdoms
Of sense, and, dominant as a cloud,
The obsolete map of chapels.
God, a crabbed shepherd of a misty path,
Whistled a thunderclap of truth.

'Poem'

36b

37a

37c

37. 'What is it that begins, or ends, in this room at midnight? A tree grows in the dark. So we easily say; but which of us can conceive of the terrors and thrustings that ever-nocturnal growing and stirring to grow involve? Who has heard the scream of the tortured roots? Or felt himself drenched and drowning in the torrent of the sap?

The wind brings us no answers
Who has heard love dying in
the dark?
It dies with the same soundless
scream as the tree utters in
its growing.
We are all deaf to that scream.'

'Love Dies as a Tree Grows'

37b

38. Harri, aged 7.

39. At school, where pupils sat three to a desk and speaking Welsh was
severely punished, Harri (front left) was regarded as a loner and was
sometimes bullied. Yet, encouraged by his mother and his teacher, Miss Lewis,
Harri read all the books in the school library.

A small boy in a small Welsh school
Dreamed over books that he would go to sea,
Knew schooners, barques, and brigantines,
The names of sails and rigging,
Dreamed of being a captain, proud and almighty,
Pacing the quarterdeck, and taming
Weather and mutiny with eyes reflecting
Glitter of seas, the seas
Of all the world—he knew them all.

'Lucky Jonah'

40. Harri, aged 8 (front right).

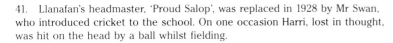

41. Llanafan's headmaster, 'Proud Salop', was replaced in 1928 by Mr Swan, who introduced cricket to the school. On one occasion Harri, lost in thought, was hit on the head by a ball whilst fielding.

'Gradually I formed for myself an adequate carapace of indifference to the ordinary world . . . and lived more and more in a world of dreams into which even Salop's hazel stick could not penetrate . . . My life became a continuous dream; my only contact with reality was my grandfather, and I was never sure where dream ended and reality began. It did not matter.'

'My Grandfather would have me be a Poet'

... *We ran, between the trees and the trees,*
Five children hand-in-hand, afraid of God,
Afraid of being among the lightning-fetching
Trees, soaked, soaked with rain, with sweat, with tears,
Frightened, if that's the adequate word, frightened
By the loud voice and the lambent threat,
Frightened certainly of whippings for being late,
Five children, ages six to eleven, stumbling
After a bit of running through trees from God.

'A Storm in Childhood'

43a

43b

43.   In 1932 the Jones' tenancy of Cwm Crogau ended and Harri's third sister, Valerie, was born. Thomas and Mary Jones moved to Rhiwolau, on the other side of Allt-y-clych (43a) leaving Llew and Ruth to take the tenancy of Trefelyn (43b), a landless Llysdinam cottage, near Allt-y-clych. Having seen the cottage, Harri told his excited sisters that they had close neighbours.

44. The family's possessions were moved down the valley by horse and 'gambo'.

'. . . It was when they began to load the gambo that Huw, who could not imagine and did not desire a life anywhere else, began to cry. Now the loading was almost finished. On the gambo were their table and two chairs, a mattress and a bundle of bedding, a lamp, Iago's axe, pots and pans, a wooden box containing food, another of china and cutlery, a tea-chest of clothes.'

'Home'

45. Life eased a little for Ruth, shown here with Harri and her three daughters. Supportive neighbours appreciated her unflagging efforts for her family, whilst Llew continued to spend every Saturday afternoon preparing for an evening at the Red Lion Inn. Children locally saw Harri as a bookish boy and called him 'Harri Palethorpe' as he would only eat a certain brand of sausage.

46a

46b

46.   The annual events of the chapel year were Pisgah 'Anniversary', the Eisteddfod and the summer visit to the seaside.

'It was a pale morning in May. For the first time in its history the Sunday School was going on an outing to the seaside. There had been a lot of opposition to the projected trip: many of the older members had felt that journeys to the seaside or anywhere else were very well for coalgrimed and contaminated chapels from down the valleys; but for Pisgah, so high in the hills it was kept clean by the wind issuing straight from the mouth of God, a tea on the Chapel Meadow in full view of the admonishing and decorous gravestones was all that was required by way of concession to the spirit of youth and its demand for some sort of a nibble at the fleshpots of Egypt. But in the end youth and progress had won the day: Pisgah must not be out of the fashion, a charabanc had been engaged, and the faithful were going to Aberystwyth for the day.
   Aberystwyth! The name made Gwilym puppy-sick with delight. Those resonant and hissing syllables spelled out for him the sea, the great mystery of blue waters covering the face of the earth and holding the wonders of the Lord, the sea which he loved so passionately and which he had never seen. . .
   . . . They were on the crest of the last hill. Standing, and peering ahead, hands gripping the seat in front of him, like a captain on his bridge, Gwilym saw the horizon as a thin strip coloured like the blade of a scythe just after sharpening. . .
   The day, the wonderful day, degenerated. It had started to drizzle; and to Gwilym's disenchanted eyes the town looked much like any other, of the few towns he had seen, only bigger. There was nothing at all to interest him in the ordinary succession of streets, houses, shops, people. . .
   . . . He despised the purchases of other children — the sweets and icecream, the coloured and lettered rock, the gimcrack toys, the balloons, the hooters, the comic postcards. His money was a mockery to him, like a stone given to a hungry man who had asked for bread. There was nothing here for him: all he wanted was the sea which no money could buy, and his dreams of the sea which no disappointment could kill.
   All the same he would like to spend the money. And suddenly, on two adjacent counters, he saw exactly what he wanted: a shiny blue notebook costing one penny and a square red *New Pocket Dictionary of the English Language*, price 6d. To the disgust of the other children Gwilym bought these two articles, and for the rest of the day he hugged them closely to his side, deriving comfort from them. . .'

'A Day at the Seaside'

46c

47a

47b

47. In 1936 Harri was the only child from Llanafan to pass the examinations for Builth Wells County Secondary School. On Mondays, Llew walked with his son to Newbridge-on-Wye where Harri caught the 6 a.m. train to Builth. Because Harri lodged in Builth during the week, he took with him 2/- and provisions for his breakfast and tea — the girls' cookery class provided the mid-day meal. Harri's lodgings, at Westbury and Hampton House in Builth, were paid for by the Council.

48. Broad Street, Builth Wells.

48

Broad St. Builth Wells

49

49. Harri enjoyed his time at Builth School. Despite his comparative poverty he became close friends with Donald Jones, the son of a local solicitor, and Robson Davies, the headmaster's son, whose home Harri visited frequently.

50. Harri (front right) portrayed Puck in the school's production of *A Midsummer Night's Dream.*

50

51. Harri (second from right, back row), in the Builth County School rugby team, 1937-8.

THE STAND-OFF HALF

They asked me to play in a Rugby
    team,
So I gave a sort of laugh
And said I would, and they answered
    "Good,
We will put you as stand-off half!"

I didn't know what they meant by that,
But I thought it was only chaff.
Still I found quite soon in the afternoon
What they meant by a stand-off half!

When fifty heavyweights form a scrum,
He stands behind like a calf,
And when they all decide to fall,
They fall on the stand-off half!

When dozens of forwards surge along
To attack on their side's behalf,
The other attack just heaves them back,
On top of the stand-off half!

The rules of the game are rather vague,
But I think that the team or staff
Don't trouble at all about goals or ball —
They play with the stand-off half!

At the end of the game I crawled away,
My head tied on with a scarf,
And I vowed in pain that never again
Would I figure as stand-off half!

HENRY JONES, FORM Va

(from The Wyeside, Builth County School magazine)

52a

52.   Harri was totally unmusical, studied French rather than Welsh, and his interest in English literature developed rapidly: he would spend many hours with Donald discussing poetry in their favourite haunt, the well-heated waiting room of Builth Wells Great Western Railway Station.

52b

53. On one occasion, Harri was
expelled from school for smoking in
Jane's parlour, a café on the Groe. His
mother was determined that Harri
should complete his education and
successfully argued his case with the
headmaster.

54a

Builth, Buallt, spa of no renown,
But sprawled about the grassy Groe,
Along the brawling reaches of the Wye,
Where I'll go home to die.

'Builth Wells'

54b

55. Throughout his school life Harri contributed his own poetry and stories to *The Wyeside*, the school magazine, and in the sixth form became its editor. By this time Harri was thinking of himself as a poet.

'The hills are very old, yet they are ever new. Always when I see them I am filled with an indescribable feeling of eternal mystery and wonder. Nothing in all this beautiful land of Wales is quite so beautiful, so ancient, so wonderful as the hills that everywhere look down with a smile on the Welshman's home.

To one born and bred in the Welsh hills their very names read like some beautiful poem or "serve in place of a prayer". This poem or prayer is endless and every true Welshman knows it by heart, and the little familiar hills of his home mean more to him than the great peaks of Snowdon and Plynlimon. So have I grown to love Allt-y-clych, from whose rocky summit one can see many miles of pleasant countryside around, and Drum Ddu, black and forbidding, where they still cut peat, and many others which it would be tiresome to repeat, since none can know them as I do.'

'The Welsh Hills', Henry Jones,
Form VI

55a

55b

56. In 1934 Ruth's fifth child was born. Harri named her Patricia Ruth.

57. Harri frequently visited his grandparents at Rhiwolau.

A little woman was dead, a little old woman
Who had long confused me with her youngest son.
I did not even think, How small she looks.
And certainly had no thoughts for her life of labour,
Nor wondered how she who had always been old to me
Had once been whatever beauty the world has
To the old man I now led out of the room,
Out of the house, up the narrow road,
In the dawn he could not see for tears, taking
My hand in his as he'd done when I was small,
Both of us wordless against the dawn and death.

'My Grandmother Died in the Early Hours of the Morning'

58. Harri's sisters would see him at weekends when he always seemed to have a book in his hand. Family life revolved around Harri — he was the apple of his mother's eye. When the rest of the family retired to bed, Harri would stay up reading by candle-light in his downstairs room.

58a

58b

59. A letter from Harri to his sisters (1945):

59

Then, my dears, for variety's sake,
I'd get up and down would take
Some old book from the shelves above,
Full of those poems that you love,
And you would read with eyes a-glisten,
While I would sit and smoke and listen.

60a

60b

60. Robson and Donald frequently visited Trefelyn: the boys would tickle trout in the Hirnant brook and occasionally go camping. During the long summer holidays Harri worked on the farm of a friend, Dai, at Dolfallen in the Elan Valley.

The trouble is, I worked with Dai, year
After year: milk bottles round the town,
Torn timber lugged down cold and bleeding hillsides,
Wet, ravaged barley ripping the skin beneath the skin,
Kale and turnips cold gifts for fingers
Without feeling, cold and mudded rods of potatoes,
Maggoty sheep in August which you had to dress
Smartly in as long as you could hold your breath.

'Welsh Pastoral Elegy'

60c

61. Llew hoped that his son would become a clerk with Breconshire County Council. However, on leaving school, Harri obtained a county exhibition scholarship to the University College of Wales, Aberystwyth, where he began his studies in October 1939, after the outbreak of war.

61b

61a

62a

62b

62a.   Harri (second from the right in the second row) was a member of the
University Dining Club.

62b.   Harri at Aberystwyth.

63. Ruth, delighted with Harri's success, sent him parcels of her home-made apple tarts and warned him to have nothing to do with actresses and not to take up boxing. Harri ignored her advice, and became a member of the college boxing team, yet, paradoxically, he canvassed vigorously in support of the anti-war movement in the college as secretary of the University Labour Club.

63a

63b

64

64. During term-time Harri supplemented his small grant by selling newspapers and playing poker. In his vacation at home Harri (right) painted for a local builder and 'tushed' timber with his cousin, Afan (middle) from Bwlchciliau.

65. Harri, with his grandfather and family.

When the cataracts came down, he remembered.
Was sometimes peevish, liked to talk in Welsh,
Was for the most part content with his old dog,
Blind, deaf, rheumatic, and pretty daft,
His firm stick, strong pipe, his memories—and me:
His grandson who could not speak his language,
Lacked his mountain skills, but in whom
He had a thorny faith not to be beaten
Down by any wind or language.

'My Grandfather Going Blind'

65

66a

66. During the war, Llew served in the Llanafan Home Guard: the closest he got to active service was when he was shot at by a jealous member of his own platoon — Llew had stripes. Harri volunteered for the Navy in the Autumn of 1941 — it was the only time Brenda and Myra saw their father cry. Harri saw his inability to swim as an asset: he would rather die quickly than swim for hours and drown anyway.

66b

67

67. The war did little to change Llanafan, but it affected all the Jones family: they are seen here together for the last time, in 1942.

68a

68b

68. Brenda joined the WRAFs and Myra the Land Army. Llanafan had no air-raid shelter (bombs fell in the area on only one occasion) — the school children would dive under the hedge equipped with gas masks during air-raid practice. Valerie and Pat always chose 'Eternal Father Strong to Save' as their school hymn.

69

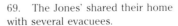

69. The Jones' shared their home with several evacuees.

70

70.   In the Navy Harri trained as a telegraphist. He wrote to his family from *H.M.S. Scotia*, a shore-based Signals School near Ayr in Scotland early in 1942:

'Dear Mam & Dad & All

We are very busy this week doing our final exams. I am doing alright in them so far. We shall be busy next week, too, getting ready for drafts. I think I am going to Portsmouth. Mind to send the clothes so that they get here by Wednesday. If you do send them don't forget a piece of navy blue or black cloth for me to patch my trousers with. It's snowing again so I don't want to walk around with holes in my trousers.

   Mick and I were lucky enough to have a free night out on Monday. We went to the theatre.

        Love to everybody

        Harry'

During the war Harri changed his signature from Harry to Harri.

After Harri's final leave before sailing from England he was based at H.M. Signals School at Petersfield:

'I've done all sorts of jobs since I've been here except the one I've been training for for the last six months. I even had the job of working a horse and cart the other day, when we were shifting some huts, and I was the only bloke who'd ever been near a horse. It was a grand job, compared to some we get, and I wouldn't mind having it every day. I've also been a sentry in the middle of the night. Tonight I'm going to the pictures in camp. We only get two nights a week, and as it only costs 3d it makes a nice, cheap change.'

71. Harri sailed from England in the spring of 1942 on the destroyer *H.M.S. Airedale*, for Africa and the Mediterranean. He was overseas for more than two years and throughout the time he was abroad wrote regularly to his family. The letters are full of enquiries about Llanafan, and comments on home news and hints of *hiraeth*. But of course, he could say little of his own activities, because of censorship.

'H.M.S. Airedale, April 1942
I love being at sea, though I wonder when I shall see you all again. I'm afraid it won't be for a very long time. We have a very free and easy time, but life is dull at sea when you have nothing to do. We can get plenty of chocolate in the canteen, and fags are 10 for 4d and beer 4½d a pint. We are only allowed 2 pints a day by the way, so you don't have to worry about me being sober.'

The Jones family at Trefelyn, having recently acquired their first wireless, heard the news of the sinking of the *Airedale* on June 15th, 1942, by a German aircraft north of Sollum, off the Egyptian coast and feared Harri had been lost.

. . . I saw a ship go down,
Quietly in the middle of the afternoon,
And thought, "That's one man will never play cards again
With confident fingers and goalscoring eye.
He loved football and cards and girls — but had to die."

'Lucky Jonah'

72. Luckily, while in Alexandria, Harri had transferred to *H.M.S. Seaham*, a small minesweeper which carried the pennant number J123 — Harri called it 'the red ship'.

71

72

73a

73b

73. On several occasions Harri met friends from home in the ports around the Mediterranean: Donald Jones (a), Ned Hughes (b) and Elwyn Davies (c), who was killed by a car when on leave in Newfoundland.

73c

And then to hear my name in a brazen bar
in Alexandria
                  (sailors in white duck escaping
From the copper sun and memories)
My name spoken by a schoolfellow
Who had come so far and — "Yes, sunk twice" —
And so was going home. And twelve months later
Killed by a motorcar in Newfoundland.
O ships we dreamed of when we both were boys,
And saw the sea once anually when the Sunday School
Charabanced us chorally to the gold coast
Of Wales and all our longings.
                  You indeed went down
To the great waters—and came back again,
Not once, but twice, and so one would have thought
Had earned the right to go back home and garden,
And grow garrulous with memories over beer,
But the car got you, certain as a shark.

'Lucky Jonah'

74. 'H.M.S. Seaham, August 1942/February 1943

I have played football for the ship a few times lately, and also done some boxing on board . . . The kids will love this. I bought myself a pair of khaki shorts, and as they were much too long, I cut the bottoms off, turned them up and sewed them. I can hear them laughing at the thought of me sewing, but I can assure them I didn't laugh. As you can imagine it took a long time, and I was thoroughly sick of it when I finished . . . I am sending a little snap for you. It is Ron, Ollie and myself, and it was taken in the rest camp we went to about four months ago. Ollie is the middle one. Don't we look happy?'

74

The patient erotic sea surrounds us
                                    always.
The tawny lands reject our wistfulness,
Sun's kiss and hammer
Press our memories
To dark corners, to elusive fields.

Neither heroic nor lucky we take our
                                    turn
In the corrupted patterns of the war.
The indifferent tides
Perhaps will heal or hurt
The already lost, the impatient
                              drinkers.

'Mediterranean: Wartime'

75. '*H.M.S.Seaham*, September 1942

You seem to have done very well at the whinberry picking. Wish I could be there to eat some of those tarts. . . I was going to send the kiddies a present, but failed to find anything suitable so please give tham five shillings each out of my extra allotment for Christmas.

Sure, you can let Afan have my sports coat, as I expect it will be a long time before I wear anything of that sort again. Tell Afan I'll have some beer off him in the Mid Wales for it when I see him next.

I have just been asked to teach a couple of the officers as much French as I know. I have accepted because, though I don't know if I can do it, I believe in having a try. It ought to be quite interesting and a very good experience for me.

. . . Ronnie and I had our photo's taken in our white duck suits (the ones we go ashore in) the other day.'

Ronnie was one of the few people who, after a few drinks, was allowed to hear the poetry Harri was writing.

All moods, all colours, blue, white, green, slate,
These are the matters of my celebration,
The moods and colours of all generation,
Fountain of birth and of man's glaucous fate.

'Moods of the Sea'

76.   Harri (fourth from the left in the front row), in Bethlehem, 1942

'*H.M.S. Seaham*, December 1942
Jerusalem was really wonderful. The town is built on four hills, and the surrounding countryside is very wild. In places on the bus ride there and back I could almost imagine myself going over the Beacons. There isn't much beer in Jerusalem, but there is plenty of wine, which you can buy quite cheaply by the bottle.'

*Drinking in bars around the sunlit
harbours
My randy ghosts, persistent as coral,
Are muted in a dream
Of sulky, reluctant seasons,
An innocent world, another time than
this.*

*Their passionate questions are dimly
answered
By forgotten girls in this perpetual
summer.
Reading in classic albums,
Only the wine-reek bears
Time and the unregenerate dream
away.*

'Mediterranean: Wartime'

76

77

77. 'H.M.S. Seaham, April, May, July 1943

I received your snaps safely the other day and was very pleased with them. I think you all look very well and happy, which is a nice thought for me. But my! how you two are growing up! But the old grey cat looks just the same . . . It was lovely hearing about the nice Spring you are having, when we hardly know if we are standing on our heads or on our feet. I would most certainly like to see those lambs and leaves and grass and birds that you talk about . . . We saw two ships sail for home the other night, with all the lads on deck cheering like mad, and, as you can easily imagine, it nearly broke our hearts, since it is almost certain that we shall have to do another year at least out here.'

A wind blew, warm as loving, from
                                    the west
And the girls came out like berries. The
                                    old hedgerows
Were sprung and blossomed to life,
                                    and could not rest
Till the hawthorn was subdued by one
                                    torn rose.

'Late Spring in Wales

78. '*H.M.S. Seaham*, July, 1943

It is Sunday morning and there is just the same air of quiet around, as there is on a Sunday morning in summer at home; though perhaps this peaceful atmosphere is somewhat deceptive here! It is already quite warm, and by the time I go on watch again this afternoon it will be really hot.

I like the sunlight but I wish I could exchange this heat for a nippy frost. One is continually thinking with longing of the cold, clear water at home . . . I often fancy a salad like we used to have with nice bread and butter, and tea out of the pot . . . I have now read all the Brecon and Radnors that you sent me and found them very interesting.'

In July 1943 *H.M.S. Seaham* was involved in the invasion of Sicily. *H.M.S. Seaham* captured an Italian submarine, and many of the badly wounded, including the German Captain, were rescued.

One day we caught a submarine, trapped like a fish
In the relentless circle of sixteen ships.
She ran the white flag up, and still our gunners
Pressed their automatic fingers
To make her run with blood. Later, we laid
The wounded on our upper deck—one was dying—
"Like a butchered sheep," I thought,
And though I tried for it, I had no pity.

'Lucky Jonah'

79a

79b

79c

79. '*H.M.S. Hannibal*, Algiers, June, July 1944

You will be pleased to hear that I am feeling fine and brown now. Usually when we go bathing, the sea is as smooth as glass, but today it was quite rough, really big breakers. This made a change and was quite good fun, but we didn't stay in very long.

It's funny to think of it being shearing time now back home, because it's so long since I have really seen sheep. I have seen them, even here, but it's only an occasional specimen, rather as one might see a goat at home, and never a flock, and anyway a sheep on a lead in the street with an Arab at the other end of the lead is very different from a sheep on the hillside at home . . .

The weather is just the same here. It will probably be monotonously glorious from now till October in all probability. I haven't been on the beach for a few days, but will be going again soon. Yes, I can manage to do a few strokes now.'

. . . and the helpless poets remain
Landfast within their private kingdoms
Of despair and pain, in terror making
Visions of love and beauty, and destroying
The value of each unending word
In the demoded vocabulary of promise.

'The Vocabulary of Promise'

80. Harri left the Mediterranean and joined *H.M.S. Westminster* off the coast of Norway.

'. . . Every day brings good news now and there are grounds for hoping that it may not be so very long now before the war is at last over, and we can all go back to the ways of peace again. Which is the fervent hope of every one of us.'

80a

80b

*So to the dear land back I sing my own
Welcome, and in my tumbling pride
Hear it re-echoed by the rain-washed winds.
Wales wears an air, a grace, as a loved face
Motions to kisses on the letters of exile;
And the intricate maps of farms
Welcome me back to a singing service,
A wonder of work, and the toil of love
In the green cathedrals of the sea-lapped,
Lovely, enduring landscape of fact and legend.*

'In My Returning'

81a

81.   Whilst waiting to be demobilised, Harri taught English at a naval base in Sheerness where he met Madeleine Scott, a WREN who taught ceramics. In the autumn of 1946, Harri returned to Aberystwyth and Madeleine to Camberwell Art School, to resume their studies. Later that term, when Harri informed his mother at Trefelyn that he intended to marry Madeleine, Ruth said, 'You can't marry, you've never had a job.' Despite Ruth's protests, they married in December 1946 and shortly afterwards they visited the Scott family in Aberdeen.

A century or kiss ago
The generations in her eyes
Answered my urgency of prayer.
Now with the words I do not know
The vision in the random air
Of absence casually dies.

'Poem for Madeleine'

81b

81c

82.   In the autumn of 1946 Harri's first published poem, 'The Enemy in the Heart', appeared in the *Welsh Review*. In 1947 he obtained a First Class Honours Degree in English and began to read for an M.A. on the metaphysical poets. Rachel 'Ray' Roberts, also a student at Aberystwyth, had her first starring role in Harri's experimental verse play, *The Weasel at the Heart*. Harri was active in the Marxist-dominated Socialist Society and edited the university magazine, *The Dragon*.

The moment has gone by
When I could have stared
Unwinking in your eye,
And with assurance dared
To love you till I die.

'For Rachel'

83

83.   Whilst reading for his M.A. on
the metaphysical poets, Harri spent
much of his time in Borth, a few miles
up the coast from Aberystwyth,
staying with his writer friend
Ted Richards.

How can I stop that shouting in my ears
Of the cold waves that batter on the rocks
Of Wales with the sound to which my own heart knocks
And all my fathers howling down the years?

O ships, o winter, o remorseless rhymes,
Let me still howl against that western sea
The old cry of the defeated and the free
For all my fathers' eloquent times and crimes.

'Prayer to the Steep Atlantick Stream'
(for the natives of Borth)

84.   Harri would go out fishing with
Ted in his boat before returning to
drink, read poetry, talk and sort out
post-war Wales. In Borth, Harri
worked in 'The Welsh Kitchen' owned
by Ted's brother, Jack, who saw Harri
as 'one of the wildest men ever to
come out of Wales'. Jack, amused by
Harri's gold tooth, was told that it
would guarantee him a few drinks on
a rainy day.

84a

84b

84c

84d

85a

85b

85.   In 1948 Harry and Madeleine's first daughter, Sian, was born. Harri and Sian joined the Jones family to celebrate 'Crogau's' ninetieth birthday, at Crossroads, Llanafan.

Grandfather, our predicament we share:
We have the nicked involvement of our name.
I try to fill your chair with all my shame.

'With a Distant Bow to Mrs Hemans'
(I.M. Tomos Jones Crogau)

85c

86

86. Harri obtained his M.A. in 1948 and felt he was on his way to a successful academic career. But the post-war period was a difficult time for aspiring working-class academics. He spent much of the time in London with Madeleine.

'Keeping the wolf, if not from the door, at least off the table by doing some part-time tutoring — teaching English to foreigners — Siamese, Persians, Swiss and French. Quite interesting and easy money, though not enough of it.'

87

87. Harri and Sian

88.   An artist friend in London, John Glanville, sculpted Harri's head. John's wife, Delia, who was studying bookbinding, presented Harri with the leatherbound 'Black Book' into which Harri transcribed all the fair copies of his poetry, until it was finally filled in 1964.

Harri wrote to the Richards':

'Your invitation to visit Borth has dug up my buried hiraeth, and I feel it was time I was wild and Welsh again.'

I sit, trying to look nonchalant,
As if I'm used to being a painter's model,
As if I'm paid or famous or beautiful,
And as I sit, while your small skilled hands
Make only a painting out of me, I am
Abashed, not only at my own inept
Pickers and stealers, but at my indolence,
So often satisfied only to think of poems.
  In the mirror I see a face
  You have not seen in any place.

'On Having My Portrait Painted'

89

89. Harri with his mother and daughter, Sian, at Trefelyn, 1949.

A woman seemed a woman
In wood or meadow
In the hard young days
When with my shadow
I moved alone.

And God was a loud voice
More urgent than thorn
There in the stoned acres
Shouting to warn
Me, me alone.

No finch now, no hazel,
Only the thorn,
God's shout a whisper,
One woman alone
Cries I was born.

'To My Mother'

90. In 1951, after two years of failing to find a university post in either Wales or England, Harri (second right, seated) settled for teaching apprentices at the Royal Naval Dockyard School in Portsmouth. Harri was a good disciplinarian whose down-to-earth approach, openness and humour made him popular with the apprentices. Many were from working-class families, and the college gave them their first opportunity of a career — something Harri could relate to.

91. Harri (extreme right), marking examination papers.

92a

92b

92.   The Jones' settled into suburban life in Battenburg Avenue, where Rhiannon was born in 1953 and Ruth in 1954.

Let her, like the sea,
All her life retain
Grace of body and mind
No accident can smutch.
As even the winter bough
Recalls its glory of leaf,
Let her, in spite of grief,
Stay beautiful as now.

'Sunday on the Beach'
(for Rhiannon)

92c

92d

92e

93

94

94. Their house was always open to friends, students and aspiring writers to eat, drink and to hear the deep, booming voice of Harri reading his poetry.

Proletarian lovers know
In their own desired park
Only the keepers come and go
In a routine to-and-fro
After dark.

For the State must still ensure
Even in such lusts divine
That rutting comrades still make sure
That their passions keep the pure
Party line.

'Workers of the World, Unite'

Remembering today the land from which
You come, the huddled nonconformist hills,
The short grass sweetening the mountain sheep,
The stubborn ponies proof against the weather,
A shepherd's hazel stick and favourite bitch,
(My best-loved image of remembered Wales)
I watch you in your curled exotic sleep,
Waywardly growing, already another stranger.

'Out of Wales'
(A Poem for my Daughter)

95

95. Harri was now calling himself a 'poor man's Dylan Thomas', and through his work with the W.E.A. encouraged young writers, one of whom was Robert Morgan, ex-miner and fellow exiled Welsh writer. Robert frequently visited Battenburg Avenue:

'Sometimes I would catch Harri deep in thought, and, when I spoke to him he would answer irrelevantly and then immediately say, "I'm sorry, I wasn't listening." I knew then I had intruded during the minting of a poem. In those days he used to read my efforts at writing poetry. He was a kind critic, choosing words to encourage never to dishearten. I remember his saying to me, "A poem must be written in a special language. No one can help you much to create this special language. But you will know when you have it."'

96. Harri, Rhiannon and Ruth on the Isle of Wight, 1956.

97. Harri, home on holiday, 1956.

96

97

98.   In the 1950's Harri read his poetry on the Third Programme and his work was regularly published in literary magazines. In 1957 Rupert Hart-Davis published his first collection of poetry, *The Enemy in the Heart*. Harri was also anxious that Hart-Davis should publish a collection of his short stories about 'Gwilym', a boy from the hills who became a famous poet. Hart-Davis was encouraging but the book was never published.

In August 1958 Harri pursued his developing interest in American literature by attending the Salzburg Seminar. He wrote to the Richards' in Borth:

'I am gloriously drunk with sunshine, wine, talk, the company of other poets, beautiful women, no responsibilities, in short, having a wonderful time.'

He met Italian Poet, Roberto Sanesi, whose poems he translated for part of his 1960 collection, *Songs of a Mad Prince*. In Salzburg Harri probably made the contacts which secured him a lectureship in English at the Newcastle College of the University of New South Wales, Australia. Harri wrote to his parents:

'We are going to Australia for a few years. I have got a job in a University out there. It is a much better job than my present one in all ways — more interest, more money, and better prospects, and university teaching is what I have always wanted to do.'

99

100

99. The *Oceania*, on which Harri and his family sailed to Australia in 1959.

'When we told the children on the morning I got the letter that we were going to Australia Ruth said, "We'll have to hurry up and eat our breakfast then"; and ever since she has been going around telling everybody that she's going on a big ship.'

On the day before Harri sailed away, Robert Morgan went to his house to say farewell. 'The house was almost empty of furniture and Harri was sitting on one of the remaining packing-cases writing a poem. He appeared to be using the poem to stifle his emotions. I said farewell, shook his hand and left him to his poem. That was the last time I saw him.'

100. Harri's children in Australia.

101.   Newcastle, a nineteenth-century convict colony, was seen in 1959 by
Harri 'as a great sprawl of a place — a bit like South Wales now and again, with
coal pits and railway lines, and lots of ponies and rugger pitches around every
corner'. Palm trees grew in the sun beside the slag heaps, vineyards rolled up
the hills beyond the pits whilst lakes and eucalyptus forests interrupted the
spread of the city.

102a

102b

102.   Harri and his family lived in a house near King Edward Park, and they felt Newcastle was going to be a good place to live, although Harri could not avoid a passing reference to *hiraeth* in his first letter to his old friends the Richards' in Borth. He also sought assurance 'that the land of my fathers still goes its dear old methodistic, alcoholic, poetic way, that there are still pubs and preachers and Spanish lady stories, and talk and scandals and a steady illegitimacy rate, and most important Richards' for me to dream of coming back to'.

But here the sun is warm on belly and back
As I indulge in wine and memories
And hear above the long Pacific swell
Stern voices of my fathers saying I lack
Their faith, their courage, their black certainties . . . .

'Wales — New South Wales. May 1961'

103

103. The University College of Newcastle was experiencing a period of rapid expansion and was regarded as a progressive institution. Harri's first reaction was uncertain, being unsure whether he would take the 'transformation into a University Lecturer as a duck to water . . .' but on reflection he added: 'I reckon I'm going to like it all right.' Amongst his colleagues Harri (front left) found a garrulous Irishman who liked whisky, rugby and Yeats; the head of the Arts Department was a Welshman, Brin Newton-John; and there was 'a wonderful exra-mural department in the shape of one Jim Dodd, wineshop proprietor and purveyor of booze to the staff. I went to his shop yesterday for the first time to place an order and in a short time had had about $\frac{1}{3}$ of a bottle of scotch in his office as well as wine samples. This is called creating goodwill. We buy sherry by the half gallon at 12/- and red wine at 6/- the half gallon.'

On a birthday card to his mother Harri quotes another friend, Professor Dai Phillip's view of Australia: 'it's not bloody Wales, boy.'

104

104.   Harri (second row, second from the right) soon found himself 'very busy with reviews, articles, WEA on top of my lecturing. All very good fun and keeps me off the drink — part of the time anyhow.'

Songs of a Mad Prince, which contained only a few Australian poems, was published in 1960 and although the reviews were patchy this seemed to stimulate a period of intense creativity, professional success and family happiness.

105.   'Sian is very pleased with herself because she won a prize in riding classes in the gymkhana on Friday. Non is all of a sudden a big girl and Ruth as always a small monkey.'

105

106. Harri (right) with A.D. Hope, 1961.

'I have astonishingly been promoted to Senior Lecturer and I am this year Acting Head of the English Department. Do you know A. D. Hope's poetry? He agreed with me that we are the two best Australian poets. (Does this sound familiar Pam?) . . . By the time you get this you will I hope have seen my first book. I distinguish between this and volumes of poetry which happen. The book is on Dylan in the 'Writers and Critics' series written by invitation and I suppose it means I can't come back to Wales — that you recognise is all balls — I am only angling — I only want the Richards' to tell me what I feel myself — this is the best book yet written on Dylan . . .

I also have coming out soon my third and best volume of poems *The Beast at the Door.* It has a superb pair of bookends, Lucky Jonah . . . and another bloody long Welshman at the other end. . .

I'm the poor colonials' Dylan Thomas now — lots of public readings. A week ago we did a reading of *Under Milk Wood*, packed houses, a great success. Appropriately after the party I fell down my own steps and cracked or broke a rib or ribs.'

107a

107. Ayer's Rock and Allt-y-clych.

For his 'daughter of the Mabinogion name', Harri wrote of her wish on her seventh birthday to ride to Ayer's Rock on a camel.

Would the vision of that monolith
Stay in her mind and dominate her dreams
As in my mind and dreams these thirty years
There stays the small hill, Allt-y-clych,
The hill of bells, bedraggled with wet fern
And stained with sheep....

'Rhiannon'

107b

108a

108b

108. In reply to a letter from Aneirin Talfan Davies, Harri wrote:

'You ask if I might come back. In many ways I'd like to — though I'd probably stop writing hiraeth-laden poems then. I like the sun, but it's not only the congeniality of life that keeps me here. I came here in the first place because I could get an academic job — this, like convicts in the old days, tends to be a one-way traffic. And of course my children, despite their Welsh names, are thoroughly Australian.'

Will you, when you are seventeen, say, or twenty-seven,
Be resentful of your sisters who had more poems?
Will you say, "Thank God, he left me alone"?
Or, "Poor father, he really couldn't help it"?

'Ruth Myfanwy'

But now—three tall daughters growing taller
Every day—who am I to boast I bear
Such tall and triple responsibility?
I should be frightened, I should run away
To sea, or to some childless woman's arms,
Or to writing poems in a lonely room.

Then I see your smile upon the pillow,
And, forgetting inconvenience, responsibility,
I answer as I can to your sweet asking,
And only hope these girls deserve their mother.

'A Birthday Poem for Madeleine'

109

109. Harri continued to provide 'occasional' poems for his family in Wales and wrote to celebrate the birth of Llew and Ruth's ninth grandchild.

May David be a big boy who
  Will be the biggest joy unto
His mother and his father, especially
  His Mam, who'll be
  Always the reason he
Will know what's what and who is who.

May he like proper things, and women most
And have words to say his liking in.
So, when he meets his old uncle's ghost,
We can together put our two words in:
His mother and my sister. And no host
Of bad things can stand against our good word.

'For David Jonathan'

110a

110b

A POEM
BY
T.H.JONES

NIMROD PAMPHLETS No.1 1964

110.   The reviews of *The Beast at the Door* (1963) were once again mixed but academic life was flourishing. Pursuing his interest in American Literature, Harri set up the first meeting of the Australian and New Zealand Association of American Studies and became its foundation secretary, giving a well-received paper on 'The Golden Age'. He published his notable narrative poem 'Cotton Mather Remembers the Trial of Elizabeth How' and his colleague Norman Talbot recalls how Harri had made himself poetry's PRO in Newcastle. 'For the rest of its inhabitants poetry came up on the same train from Sydney in 1959 as the small vivid Welshman called Harri . . . At a public meeting or over a private beer, poetry was part of his sustenance and his hospitality . . . Well I mean, apart from drinking and making love and arguing about rugby what else is there?'

111a

111. Harri (back to camera)
continued to write poems often 'on
small record cards in the pub at
lunch-time or in the small hours of
the morning or after a party',
externalising his own personal terrors
and fears in the poetry of the
confessional.

And though you make of me your nightly care,
Your arms around me as loving evidence
That such proximity is our best defence
Against the terrors of nightmare and nightmare,
My guilt is closer to me even than you.

'Between Nightmare and Nightmare'

111b

112a

112b

112.   Harri read his poetry in Newcastle Cathedral and now saw himself as 'Mr, the almost anonymous lecturer'.

Mr every now and again is deflected
From his marking, boredom, marking time,
To wonder momentarily if he was right
To ask of vulnerable innocence
What it thinks about the imprisonment
Of a great Prince.
                    His automatic pencil,
Cancelling an ampersand, dismisses
The futile question. He feels morally secure
Because he didn't interogate them,
Her, about her, his favourite Elegie.
At that minding of Bed's America
He resolutely goes on marking.
                              It's marking time.

'Girl Reading John Donne'

113a

I had thought to be a proud man and isolated,
Inviolate as my hills even in defeat...

And now I live in the good meadows, and I have
No emblem except your body, and I am
Still a member of a narrow chapel, and a boy
From a hungry parish, a spoiled preacher,
Greedily taking the surplus of your sunshine,
And still afraid of hell because I've been there.

'Llanafan Unrevisited'

113b

114

Should I go back then
To the narrow path, the sheep turds,
And the birded language? . . .

Of course I'd go back if somebody'd pay me
To live in my own country
Like a bloody Englishman.

But for now, lacking the money,
I must be content with the curlew's cry
And the salmon's taut belly

And the waves, of water and of fern
And words, that beat unendingly
On the rocks of my mind's country.

'Back?'

115. In 1965 Harri was looking forward to spending a sabbatical year at Columbia University, U.S.A., and visiting Wales on his return journey. On January 29th, after a particularly hard week of organising and lecturing on his pet summer school of poetry and drama, he took his regular evening walk on the cliffs overlooking the Indian Ocean. Harri, who could not swim, was found drowned that evening in the Bogey Hole, a dangerous swimming pool cut out of the rocks by convicts in the nineteenth century.

115

116a

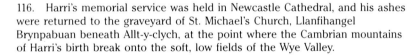

116b

116.   Harri's memorial service was held in Newcastle Cathedral, and his ashes were returned to the graveyard of St. Michael's Church, Llanfihangel Brynpabuan beneath Allt-y-clych, at the point where the Cambrian mountains of Harri's birth break onto the soft, low fields of the Wye Valley.

117.   'In Memory of Harri Jones'

From Irfon, guilty water
And up the Chwefri where
A dead prince and a dead poet
Called me, the road leads
From Epynt where all words
Fail in the witless wind.
You did well to get out of ·
This hole in the middle of Wales,
Only there is nowhere else
Anywhere. I went on:
Dylife, broken teeth
Snarling, Clywedog, a wound
Laying bare the black Silurian
Bedrock of rotten bone.
Were you perhaps lucky
Not to come back to this land
Of dead villages and ruined harvests?

Harri Webb

117

118. Ben Jones' study drawing of Cephasus.

119. Cephasus, sculpted in 1985 by Ben Jones to celebrate the poetry of T. Harri Jones.

Biographical and Bibliographical Dates

1921	T.H. Jones born at Cwm Crogau, Llanafan Fawr, December 21st
1926	Llanafan Church School
1932	Moves to Trefelyn
1933	Builth Wells County Secondary School
1939	County Exhibition Scholarship
1939	University College of Wales, Aberystwyth
1941	Volunteers for the Royal Navy, August
1946	Resumes studies at Aberystwyth, October
	First published poem 'Enemy in the Heart', *The Welsh Review*
	Marries Madeleine Scott, December
1947	1st Class Honours Degree, English
1948	Student production of *Weasel at the Heart*, February
	Sian, first daughter, born
	M.A. 'Imagery of the Metaphysical Poets'
1951-1959	Teaches English at the Royal Naval Dockyard Technical College, Portsmouth
	W.E.A. lecturer in Portsmouth and Isle of Wight
	Reads his poetry on Third Programme
	Publishes poetry, short stories and criticism in literary journals
1953	Rhiannon, second daughter, born
1954	Ruth, third daughter, born
1957	First volume of poetry, *The Enemy in the Heart*, published by Hart-Davis
1958	Attends Salzburg Seminar, Summer
1960	Lecturer in English, University College, Newcastle, New South Wales, Australia
1960	*Songs of a Mad Prince*, Hart-Davis
1961	Senior Lecturer
	Secretary of Australia and New Zealand Association of American Studies
1963	*The Beast at the Door*, Hart-Davis
	Dylan Thomas, Oliver and Boyd
1965	Drowned, January 29th
1966	*The Colour of Cock Crowing*, Hart-Davis
	T. Harri Jones Award, Newcastle University
	T. Harri Jones Prize, Builth Wells Secondary School
1976	Monograph by Julian Croft in the 'Writers of Wales' series
1977	*Collected Poems*, Gomer Press
1985	Commemorative sculpture of T. Harri Jones, by Ben Jones, Builth Wells
	Exhibition, 'Life and Times of T. Harri Jones', Wyeside Arts Centre, Builth Wells
1987	Exhibition of T. Harri Jones' life, Oriel Gallery, Cardiff

Acknowledgements

The Editors would particularly like to thank the following:

South-East Wales Arts Association, for commissioning the book.
Madeleine Mitchell, the poet's widow, for photographs and generous help.
Pam Richards for personal memories and manuscripts.
Robert Morgan for the Portsmouth years.
David Power for his down-to-earth humour.
Michael Power for his invaluable support and administrative skills.
Ioan Hurford for the map of the Hirnant and Chwefru valleys.
Donald Jones for the Builth Wells school years.
Jonathon Morgan and Wyeside Arts Centre for a focus and base for a community venture.
Isobel Thomas for the family tree.
Ben Jones for his sculpture and drawing and his assistance with our original exhibition.
Brynmor Thomas and Mr and Mrs Bill Anthony-Jones for the Aberystwyth years.
Ian Brown and Builth Wells High School for their support of the project and the loan of the lead bust of T. Harri Jones by John Glanville.
Tony Bianchi and Meic Stephens of the Welsh Arts Council's Literature Department.
Brenda Strudwick, Myra Owen and Valerie Jones, the poet's sisters, for their memories of the childhood years.
Mr E George, formerly Principal, Royal Navy Technical College, Portsmouth.
Felgate Training
Ann Hunt
Don Dale-Jones
Phil Rickman
Ronnie Roantree
Gomer Press, Llandysul, for permission to quote extensively from the *Collected Poems*.
Harri Webb for permission to quote from 'In Memory of Harri Jones'.
The people of Llanafan Fawr and Newbridge-on-Wye.

Photographs

Mo Abraham 42b
Kelvyn Curry 57a
Liz Felgate 2, 17a, 17b, 19b, 29b, 33b, 34a, 36a, 36b, 37a, 37b, 41b, 43a, 43b, 55b, 60a, 79b, 80b, 93, 107b, 113a, 113b, 114a, 116a, 117
P. Bernard Jones 14, 34b, 37b, 41c, 42a, 83, 116b
David Power 7, 16b, 54a, 60b, 92a
Robert Greetham 88a, 88b
Imperial War Museum, London 71, 78
National Library of Wales, Aberystwyth 33a, 46a, 46c, 49, 61a
Newcastle Herald, New South Wales, Australia 115
Welsh Industrial and Maritime Museum, Cardiff 13
Ruth Jones (poet's daughter), Audrey Batten, Hilda Cole, Glyn Davies, Robson Davies, Bill Hughes, Judith Hurford, Gwenda Jones, Stanley Kaye, Mrs P. Mason, Miss G. Morris-Williams, Mr R.C.B. Oliver, Jack Richards, Llew Teideman

Sources

All poems by T. Harri Jones are taken from *The Collected Poems of T. Harri Jones* (Llandysul 1977), except as indicated in the text.

The short stories are taken from the following sources:
'A Day at the Seaside', *Dock Leaves*, V, 15, Winter 1954.
'Home', *The Dublin Magazine*, XXX, 2, 1954.
'My Grandfather would have me be a Poet', *Life and Letters*, LXIV, 149, January 1950.

Pat Power, P. Bernard Jones, Liz Felgate